Photo by Sally Cookson

Paul Cookson has been writing poems for fifty years or so, publishing them for over forty years, and has had the job title of "Poet" for thirty years. He is a National Reading Hero award-winner, Poet-in-Residence for The National Football Museum and Everton in the Community, and Writer-in-Residence for Sing Together. Before lockdown in March 2020, he spent most of his time visiting schools around the country delivering workshops and performances and publishing a variety of collections for children. Since then, he's hardly been anywhere (apart from his garden or his study), but has written a poem every single day and published them on Facebook, Twitter and Instagram. Like many others, Paul now spends his time developing home cooking skills, doing the jobs he'd never got round to, walking round the block and shouting at the television. He has also spent time collaborating with a variety of other artists, songwriters and illustrators and has a new album coming out with Don Powell's Occasional Flames, *Just My Cup of Tea*. For more information you can visit paulcooksonpoet.co.uk or occasional-flames.co.uk, and you can follow his daily poems on Twitter @paulcooksonpoet.

Selected works

For adults:
Fighting Talk: A COVID-19 Poetry Diary, Vol. 1 †
Touched by The Band of Nod – The Slade Poems •
The Saturday Men •

For children:
Football 4 Every 1 ★
The Very Best of Paul Cookson ★
Paul Cookson's Joke Shop ★
There's a Crocodile in the House ◆

As Editor:
The Works ★
100 Brilliant Poems for Children ★
Fire Burn, Cauldron Bubble ▲

† Published by Flapjack Press
• Published by A Twist in the Tale & available at paulcooksonpoet.co.uk
★ Published by Pan Macmillan ◆ Published by Otter Barry Books
▲ Published by Bloomsbury

CAN OF WORMS
PAUL COOKSON

A COVID-19 POETRY DIARY
VOLUME 2

Illustrated by Martin Chatterton

Flapjack Press
flapjackpress.co.uk

Exploring the synergy between performance and the page

Published in 2021 by Flapjack Press
Salford, Gtr Manchester
⊕ flapjackpress.co.uk
f Flapjack Press ✔ FlapjackPress

ISBN 978-1-8381185-1-8

Cover & illustrations by Martin Chatterton
⊕ worldofchatterton.com
✔ MEChatterton ◎ edchatt

Printed by Imprint Digital
Exeter, Devon
⊕ digital.imprint.co.uk

FSC

MAN
CHE
STER
A UNESCO City
of Literature

*Dedicated to Les Glover,
the man who finds the melodies in the lines.*

*Thanks to all of you who comment and share online
on a daily basis – a virtual audience.
Thank you – without you …*

*Special thanks to Stewart Henderson,
good friend and fellow poet, for his sage-like wisdom,
objectivity and encouragement throughout.*

Contents

A few words – as if there haven't been enough …

Thanks to all of you bought *Fighting Talk* – Volume 1. And of course, if you are reading this, then thanks for buying Volume 2 as well. Not only is it supportive and encouraging, but it has made a huge difference. Not being able to work – go out and perform, etc – has impacted enormously and every little helps.

Already Volume 3, *Pig's Ear, Dog's Dinner*, is scheduled for later this year. I'm aiming that the last poem for this book may be on March 23rd, exactly one year since I started writing. We may still be "here" (whatever that means) and I will probably still be writing, but we thought that Volume 3 should bring us to a year of poems. Also, the day when I'll shave my beard off as well, if you're interested.

Great news too is that the wonderfully talented Korky Paul (he illustrates *Winnie the Witch* amongst other things – look him up!) is on board. I'm so looking forward to that. I've known Korky for years and whenever he's illustrated my poems before they have always been a joy to behold.

A couple of things about these poems.

They are instant responses, snapshots. Usually when writing I'd draft a poem several times, road test it in performance, draft again before putting it into print, but this project isn't like that. The very nature of "a poem a day" makes it so. That may be their weakness, but hopefully it's their charm as well.

Also, I didn't want every poem to be a grumpy old response to the situation and those in charge. Goodness knows, that was entirely possible! Obviously, some storylines and occurrences needed a specific response, but I wanted to make *my* responses varied and, hopefully, interesting in terms of style, form, tone and humour. It would be very easy to be angry and cynical all the time, but that doesn't make for interesting reading. I tried to approach it like a gig, so there's light and shade, humour, thoughtfulness and anger where appropriate. And make it personal.

One of the nicest quotes I've had is "Your diary is our diary, Paul". In a way, I think that is part of a poet's job – to be a mirror.

Posting on social media brings interesting responses, too. Glen Matlock retweeted a poem, which led to a further poem ('An Ex-Sex Pistol Retweeted My Tweet'). As did Badly Drawn Boy – which started a lovely interaction and led to Damon providing a quote for the book. Brilliant!

Talking of which – Michael Rosen … Thank you so much, Michael, for the fantastic quote. A couple of poems in *Fighting Talk* related to Michael and his COVID-19 battles. Great to have you back sir and great to hear your virtual voice.

This was going to a few words … see how that turned out!

Before I sign off, special thanks to Martin Chatterton for his illustrations and design – always brilliant, always hit the right note. With this and a few other projects, we've been in touch on almost a daily basis. Cheers brother.

As I said, *Pig's Ear, Dog's Dinner* will be out later in the year and the cover is on the last page if you want to look – which you've just done.

Take care, stay safe and stay in touch, eh?

Paul Cookson
January 2021

#115 / 03:07:2020

Anyone drinking in the pub'll
At 6 a.m. be asking for trouble

Can of Worms

Dear Prime Minister

#116 / 03:07:2020

I shan't call you "Boris"
As people may think that implies friendship
And I shan't refer to you as "Mister"
As that signifies respect

I think I'll leave out the "Dear" too

So, Prime Minister
You had a chance – a real once in a lifetime chance

You could have united the nation
With decisive leadership
Direct and immediate action
A brave and direct approach
But you just couldn't do it

You could have led the way
From a position of authority and majority
Built a legacy, something memorable
Left your opponents way behind

Imagine if you had reached out to the N.H.S. and beyond
Publicly praised them all as the jewels in our crown
And backed it up with appropriate budgets and wages structures
In making them heroes
You would have yourself been the hero maker

You could have been honest
About your chief advisor's lies
Sacked him and gained a nation's respect
You could have brought people together
Done all this and more

This door was open for you
But you dithered
Ummed and *ahhed*
Blustered and ultimately said nothing of note

It took a young footballer
To teach you empathy, heart and compassion

Prime Minister
That could have been you
That should have been you
You could have been remembered as
The People's Prime Minister
Who showed us the way in difficult times
Led us in – dare we say it – unprecedented times
You even survived the virus
You could have been a national hero
You had your chance
Amidst this can of worms you had your chance
Yet you could not take it
You could not do it
Yes, Prime Minister
You blew it

I Will Not Take the Knee

#117 / 04:07:2020

I will not take the knee
So says our brave Prime Minister
Principled, strong words
Or something much more sinister?

I will not take the knee
I don't believe in gestures
Yet still I clap the N.H.S.
Applaud all our investors

I will not take the knee
I believe in things substantial
Like capital and merchant banks
And everything financial

I must remain impartial
Unbiased and apart
No suggestion that a gesture
Is an action of my heart

But …

Your life is one big cliché
Gestures – you've made plenty
Most of them embarrassing
Pitiful and empty

You want something of substance
Not dead down in a ditch
Action – not a gesture
Says the man who hid inside a fridge

You will not bow to pressure
You will not take the knee
Unless it's to the markets
And hypocrisy

The Little Things That Make You Feel Human Again
#118 / 05:07:2020

July the fourth – Independence Day
We know the virus hasn't gone away
But doors that were locked are opening now
So we'll take care, get through somehow

Glory be – hairdressers at last!
A cut and a chat from a friend in a mask
Ordering food that you haven't prepared
The luxury of an experience shared

Pub doors open – a beer with others
A chat with a stranger, a joke with another
Feels almost normal since I don't know when
The little things that make you feel human again

Blue Sunday

#119 / 05:07:2020

Lock down to lock in – alcohol release
Suddenly we've got a breach of the police

We predict a riot – right on cue
Haven't they got better things to do?

They call it revelry and hi-jinx
Letting off steam, high spirits and drinks

Now we need the boys and girls in blue
Haven't they got better things to do?

The dangerous mix of time plus beer
Would lead to a change in the atmosphere

It all went wrong – well, who knew?
Haven't they got better things to do?

Nobody wants blue flashing lights
Bottles and flares and drunken fights

We know you've got better things to do
You serve us – we salute you

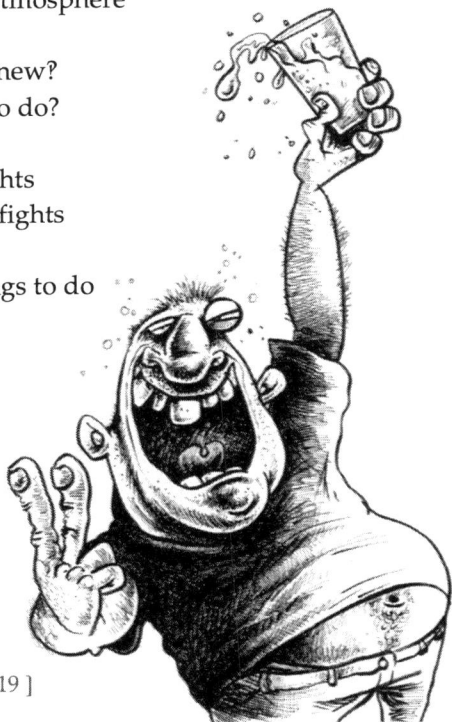

Happy Birthday and God Bless

#120 / 06:07:2020

Happy birthday – celebrate
Something that is truly great

Those who cure, those who care
Those who shoulder, those who share

Those who listen, those who give
Their lives to help all others live

Those whose patience knows no ends
Those whose patients they call friends

Those who research, those who reach
To share their knowledge when they teach

Those who've been and those who've gone
All who pass that baton on

Those we recognise, front line
Those invisible, behind

All those who we never see
Cleaning floors, making tea

Those who wash or cook the meals
Everyone who turns the wheels

Those who save, those who serve
All of those who so deserve

More than just appreciation
Applause from such a grateful nation

A wage that values contribution
To this living institution

We raise a glass, we all say yes!
Thank you for the N.H.S.

Thank God for – and God bless
Long live our N.H.S.

Five Lines of Fun and Truth

#121 / 07:07:2020

The rhyme must always fit the poem
And not vice versa
If you crowbar a rhyme just because it rhymes
It sticks out like a sore thumb and changes the rhythm of the
    line
And makes the poem worser

More Than a Soundtrack

for Ennio Morricone
#122 / 07:07:2020

"Music is an experience, not a science"
So says a maestro
And with your track record
Who are we to argue?

More than just a cowboy theme
You were always better than good
Never bad
And never ever ugly
Not afraid to experiment
Observe, listen, record and evaluate
Patience is a virtuoso
A masterpiece in waiting

The assemblance of sound
The combination of instruments
The accumulation of notes
And the spaces between them
The noise and the silence
The perfect cadence and structure
But what makes it an experience
Is the emotional connection

Art without emotion has no beauty
Music with no feeling does not touch us
Haunting melody, the luminous melancholy
Or quite simply a tune we can whistle
We may not know all your genius
We may not be able to spell your name
But we can all whistle at least one tune
As indeed we are doing right now

Shifting the Blame

#123 / 08:07:2020

Shifting the blame – always the same
A quote to confuse and deflect it
Shifting the blame – again and again
To detract, distract, misdirect it

Twisting the blame – it's part of their game
Cowardly, clumsy – at best
Twisting the blame – the lies that remain
Like the truths that remain unconfessed

Twisting the blame with unfounded claims
Yet still, no sign of retraction
Shifting and twisting the blame is their aim
To their own smug satisfaction

Shifting and twisting, resisting all blame
The lines with which they've persisted
No scruples or shame, if it's all the same
We'll blame all you shifty and twisted

Kickstart

#124 / 09:07:2020

It's not that your efforts aren't welcome
But is this where we want to be?
Trying to get back on track
Kickstarting the economy?
Looking for some sort of answer
Returning to normality
Yet still, there are questions of safety
But kickstarting the economy?

A voucher for food on the high street
Reductions on V.A.T.
All very nice – but what is the price
Kickstarting the economy?
These steps may be the direction
To rebuild society
It takes more than cash and injection
To kickstart the economy

Let's kickstart the safety in care homes
The safety of those we can't see
Kickstart the N.H.S. budgets
That's the priority
Economy is just people
Workers like you and like me
It's a kickstart – but it's only a start
If we don't see it through properly

Investment and value and fairness
Quality, equality
All should be taken account of
Kickstarting the economy

Sonnet in Praise of Creators

#125 / 10:07:2020

Forget not the creators of diversions
Those that lift our spirts and our hearts
In the spotlight or behind the curtains
Appreciate all artists and their arts

The singers of the songs and all the dancers
Those who have the gift for joy and laughter
The writers of the stories that entrance us
Once upon a time – happy ever after

Poets and the playwrights and musicians
Those who paint and sculpt and all the actors
Make belief, reality magicians
Who entertain, inspire – and distract us

Cherish them for bringing us together
For now's the time we need them more than ever

The Name Says It All

for Jack Charlton
#126 / 11:07:2020

Charlton

A word synonymous with football
World Cups and glory

For a certain age
A name that means so much

We may think of Bobby first
But always, always think of Jack in a heartbeat

We may have wanted to play like Bobby
But most of us related to Jack

Endeavour, commitment and fight
We could all be a bit like him

Big Jack at the back – knew his place
Big Jack at the back – did his job

Big Jack at the back – no-one passed
Big Jack at the back – you'd want him on your side

He once said "I couldn't play
But I could stop others playing"

Not true – but true
Uncompromising, straightforward and honest

My dad would always call him "Giraffe neck"
And if dad thought he was "good'un" then he was

In an age where heroes were ordinary
Big Jack was just that – but so much more

One-man club, total legend
Seven hundred and seventy-three appearances

Loved by those who played with him
Loved by those who played for him

The footballer's footballer
Loved by football fans everywhere

Jack Charlton
The name says it all

Mandatory Masks ... Which Sounds Like It Should Be A Concept Album Title by Rush (Which Would Be More Interesting)

#127 / 12:07:2020

Mandatory masks in Morrisons
Mandatory masks in M&S
Mandatory masks?
In shops we ask
Then the answer should be yes

Mandatory masks – a muddled mess
Mixed messages and delays
Mandatory masks?
If so, we ask
Why wait then ten more days?

More than "courtesy and good manners"
Masks are mandatory
It's now time to cover up
Like the ministers in this story

Sixty (or so) Words and Phrases That Spring to Mind When Your Football Team Has Been Utterly Embarrassed – Today It's Everton (3-0 Against Wolves, Should Have Been More), Tomorrow It Could Be Your Team

#128 / 13:07:2020

Dull and dismal – totally abysmal
Goal-less, guile-less, gut-less and spineless
No formation, no inspiration
No concentration, not even perspiration
Apathetic, non-athletic, pitiful and so pathetic
Useless, toothless – everything but ruthless
Disturbingly disjointed – more than disappointed
Out-muscled, out-tussled, feathers ruffled, out-hustled
No tackle, no bite, no snap, no fight
Boring, clueless – could they really do less?
No show, too slow, never gonna pass go
Leader-less and error strewn
Tortured in the afternoon
Nothing to be proud about
Nothing to be loud about
Nothing we can shout about
Glad there's not a crowd about
Frightened, fearful – you're gonna get an earful
Angry, disgusted, a team that can't be trusted
Utterly, completely, surrendering so meekly
Retreating in defeat-we – do it almost weekly

Heartless – art-less, totally naïve
But still we have faith, still we believe
Hopeless, dopey, the future's looking bleak
Guess what? We'll be back next week

Why oh why oh why oh why
What are we waiting for?
Why oh why oh why oh why
Delay a little more?

The virus will not go to sleep
Till July twenty-four
There's a horse that bolted long ago
And you can't find the stable door

Why oh why oh why oh why
Must we all endure
This chaos and confusion
And incompetence galore?

Up the creek without a paddle
Never mind an oar
There's a horse that bolted long ago
And you can't find the stable door

Who oh why oh why oh why
Have you chosen to ignore
Warning signs in these plague times
As numbers still they soar?

The scientists are telling us
What horrors lie in store
There's a horse that bolted long ago
And you can't find the stable door

Masks right now just shows quite how
You're drifting from the shore
Floundering and flailing
With every fatal flaw

What is it you cannot see
When we all know the score?
There's a horse that bolted long ago
And you can't find the stable door

Wear a Mask You Idiot –
At Least It'll Cover Up Your Stupid Mouth

#130 / 15:07:2020

S   ir Desmond Swayne
A   Tory name
D   eclares his opposition
T   o shopping guidelines and he claims
W   earing masks is such a pain
A   nd as such he will maintain
T   his monstrous opposition

On Being Aware

#131 / 16:07:2020

There are books of which I'm aware
In that – I know they are there
Titles of great renown
I'm aware they are around

Aware that they have been written
I read a review with a bit in
Aware of the stories – well, loosely
But the finer details confuse me

Somewhat vague about the chapters
But I think it ends happy ever after
I've seen them on someone else's shelf
But haven't read them myself

There is a reading list
So I am aware that they do exist
I'm aware of all their pages
But reading them takes me ages

Aware, not fully aware – in short
No, I haven't read that report

Effort

#132 / 17:07:2020

Sometimes it's a real effort
To get out of my pyjamas
It hardly seems worth the effort
Unless I'm doing a weekly shop

And when I do get dressed
I seem to be wearing the same clothes
Most days
No reason to do otherwise

Looking in my sock drawer
There are plenty of cheerful colours
But I can't bring myself to wear them
Not in the mood for happy socks

I've come to the conclusion
That I have underpants older than my children
(Probably more supportive and reliable too)
They have seen better days

Then again, so have I
I should really upgrade and buy new
But as someone who shops at Morrisons
Pants with weekly meat and veg doesn't seem right

And hardly worth the effort
Which reminds me
Sometimes it's hardly worth the effort
To get out of these pyjamas and get dressed

A Strong and Sincere Hope

"It is my strong and sincere hope that we will be able to review the outstanding restrictions and allow a more significant return to normality from November at the earliest – possibly in time for Christmas."

— *Boris Johnson*

That Everton will rise again
Invincible in every game
Eclipse past glories with new fame
A strong and sincere hope

That Noddy, Jimmy, Dave and Don
Will reunite for one last song
And once again be number one
A strong and sincere hope

That lottery numbers all come up
England win the next World Cup
A million sales for my next book
A strong and sincere hope

That a cure is found – and fast
Worldwide peace and joy – at last
Poverty is in the past
A strong and sincere hope

That Donald finds humility
Boris finds some honesty
And we all live in harmony
A strong and sincere hope

All the odds against are stacked
None of these are based on fact
Impossible – to be exact
A strong and sincere hope

None of us know what's in store
The future may be insecure
But we deserve so much more
Than a strong and sincere hope

A Sunday Poem

#134 / 19:07:2020

Those like-minded who have chosen to gather
With common spirit who have come together
The sanctity of song
The release of emotion

The unity of public confession
Be it church or chapel of worship
Football ground or sporting occasion
Concert hall, village hall, theatre or pub room

We miss this mass
The coming together of one accord
To share in something special
Capture the spirit within this place

The now that strengthens and uplifts
These moments shared and celebrated
Invisible electricity that connects
Blood and life and breath

Goosebumps, heartbeat and the soul
The sharing of magic
The taking away of inspiration
The fulfilment of unity

Through this
Our common union
This, our holy communion
Peace be with you ...

All We Want for Christmas is the Vaccine

#135 / 20:07:2020

It may still be the summer
When the skies are clear and blue
And the sun outside is brightly
Shining down on me and you
But we're living in the shadow
Of this COVID-19
And all we want for Christmas is the vaccine

Too far to plan ahead right now
And write a festive list
To share with friends and family
And everyone we've missed
All these season's reasons
Reality or dream?
And all we want for Christmas is the vaccine

Peace on Earth, goodwill to all
And signs that things are better
These, our wishes for the year
Written in a letter
To Santa, God, Buddha, Boris
And everyone between
All we want for Christmas is the vaccine

Never mind the baubles
Never mind the snow
With all this social distancing
Forget the mistletoe
A face mask and some hand gel
And a future that is clean
All we want for Christmas is the vaccine

You Only Get Out …

#136 / 21:07:2020

There's foreign money rushing round
In governmental coffers
Who knows what promises were made
Alongside all these offers?
As the adage goes
It's something or it's nothing
But …
You only get out what you Putin

Capital investments
From these overseas donations?
Kremlin's in the system
Overseeing situations?
Oligarchs – get on your marks
Do they want their own cut in?
Because …
You only get out what you Putin

If you follow all the money
Then you'll always find the truth
But power is corruption
So you'll never find the proof
Investigate these dealings
And the shady doors keep shutting
And …
You only get out what you Putin

Believe now all the stories – the Tories voted "yes"
To a deal on the table to sell the N.H.S.
Those who bid the highest are the ones who'll pass the test
Economy, not people but financial interest
National wealth not national health and doing what is best
Don't you dare get ill if you're poor or earning less
This national affrontery, sickening to digest
Believe now all the stories that the Tories voted "yes"

This jewel in our crown that helps those in distress
Pawned and pimped and auctioned, open to contest
Money, spin and mirrors, monopoly and chess
Checkmate and no check-ups, out-manoeuvred in this mess
Just ensure that Trump and all of the U.S.
Are as far away as possible from our N.H.S.
And when we all look back saying "goodnight and God bless"
Just remember this – the Tories voted "yes"

Looking Back

#138 / 23:07:2020

In retrospect
Looking back
I could have written this poem differently

It could have had a better opening line
And a less obvious scheme of rhyme

I could have even
Written every verse in the
Form of a haiku

But did not take the
Time and wasn't prepared to
Do all the planning

I could have edited as I went along
Redrafted and improved
Made it a work in progress

Instead, I responded
With obvious phrases and clichés

Mixing metaphors and ill-thought-out similes
This poem was like a road map of confusion
As easy to follow as dyslexic alphabetti-spaghetti

The inconsistencies in the narrative didn't help
Verses about castles distracted

And because it went on so long
People got bored

This poem became irrelevant
At one point I thought this was the poem
That might change the world

It could have been so different
This poem could have been my legacy

The power and the strength of committed words
Emotion and empathy that reached out
Touched hearts and changed lives

In retrospect
Looking back
I should have written it differently

Settled on a genre
Taken advice from those wiser than me
Learnt from the examples of others
And then created my own masterpiece
Maybe in the highlands

Instead, I often went for cheap jokes
Buffoonery and puns that went from bad to verse
I could have written so much more
And written it so much more betterly
But didn't

What We All Need Now …

#139 / 24:07:2020

Never mind that food banks are struggling to continue
Never mind that full fat food is always on the menu
Never mind obesity – here's how we can fix it
What we all need now is a fifty-pound voucher bicycle repair kit

Never mind that fast food is so readily available
Never mind the fact it's cheap makes it so retailable
Never mind that quality of life will always take a hit
What we all need now is a fifty-pound voucher bicycle repair kit

Never mind that fruit and veg is costly and expensive
Never mind that changes needed are the most extensive
Never mind all that – let's do a little bit
What we all need now is a fifty-pound voucher bicycle repair kit

Obesity has many forms – economic inequality
Some are fit and some are thin, not just what they want to be
Lose five pounds of weight, get on your bike, get fit
What we all need now is a fifty-pound voucher bicycle repair kit

The Day of the Mask Parade

#140 / 25:07:2020

The time is now, the day is here
For those who venture far and near
And safety first is crystal clear
In market or arcade
Today's the day but we all know
It should have been this months ago
Government – far too slow
For this mask parade

So … now the science has evolved
Enough for all of those involved
To think the problem could be solved
Opinions have been swayed
Don your mask and off you pop
To the pub or down the shop
Keep on spending, do not stop
In your mask parade

Has common sense prevailed at last?
Or has the time to act fast passed?
The cards are dealt, the die is cast
It seems we've all been played
And now we've found we could be fined
If we leave them all behind
So keep a spare to help remind
You of this mask parade

It's the dithering that's withering
On what you're not delivering
The time you took considering
Decisions to be made

No strategies pinpointed
Responses so disjointed
That left us disappointed
In this mask parade
In this masquerade
To mask your mass charade

Too Long

#141 / 26:07:2020

I haven't spoken to mum
For a while now
Too long

Not seen her since
The day before lockdown
Too long

She's confused
This hasn't helped
Over a hundred miles away

Might as well be the moon
Worlds apart
I'm not sure she understands

Then again
Neither do I
It's been too long

Optimistic Fizz

(After Dominic Raab's statement that our P.M.'s "optimistic fizz" would hold the U.K. together)
#142 / 27:07:2020

What ho! Hoorah! Chin chin!
It's super and it's whizz!
A leader who will lead us with his
Optimistic fizz
Optimistic fizz
Like the bubbles in champagne
That briefly sparkle, rise and pop
Never seen again
The sodastream when drinks are flat
That really is a swizz
Not like on the adverts
Optimistic fizz
The crackle when you try to tune
A radio's what it is
A damp squib of a firework
Optimistic fizz
The buzzing of a buzzer
For an answer in a quiz
That you thought was right but isn't
Optimistic fizz
Retro aftershave
To get the ladies in a tizz
Who needs Hai Karate when there's
Optimistic Fizz?
The right man for the job?
The bee's knees and the biz?
Or a snake oil selling salesman and his
Optimistic Fizz?

We need statesmanship, thoroughness, respectability
Gravitas, seriousness and diplomacy
Alas – all these won't come to pass
Not qualities of his
Just effervescent emptiness
And optimistic fizz

Coronavee the Mystery Cat

(Written after it was confirmed that a cat had contracted COVID-19 –
with apologies to T.S. Eliot)
#143 / 28:07:2020

Coronavee the hidden cat that no-one ever sees
Coronavee the mystery cat who's bound to make you sneeze
He's the bafflement of doctors and scientists despair
For when they try to find him – Coronavee's not there
Coronavee's the cat amongst the pigeons of us all
This feline leaves us feline not so well and rather small
You may see him in the market, you may see him in the square
But when you try to stop him – Coronavee's not there
Coronavee, Coronavee – there's no-one like Coronavee
Coronavee – a loner – he – can spread diseases easily
You may hear a little mewling or a distant sort of purr
But wherever you are looking Coronavee's not there
Coronavee's the secret kitty we all know is there
Maybe in the basement or maybe on the stair
Far too clever to be found by likes of you and me
The one and only viral cat that is Coronavee!

Situation Vacant

#144 / 29:07:2020

Situation Vacant – and has been for some time
Situation Vacant – sign on the dotted line
Opportunity is knocking – open up the door
If you have the qualities that we are looking for …
Wanted:
Can you speak in sentences
On a daily basis?
Charismatic with one of
Those camera-friendly faces?
Someone who's appealing
To all women and all men
Can you be the spokesperson
For those in Number Ten?
Someone analytical
Partisan political
Toe the party line and then
Mouth the words for Number Ten
Thick of skin, committed, bold
To only do what they are told
Stand and face the nation's press
Don't say no and don't say yes
Someone sharp of tongue and wit
Who understands the game
Someone who can answer questions
Directly while deflecting blame
Someone calming, non-alarming
Cool and quite collected
Unflustered and un-blustered
Someone unelected
Somebody convincing
Can lie without the wincing

Can you think while on your feet?
Unlike those in Downing Street
Take the bullets when they're fired
Do all this – then you'll be hired
All for a hundred grand a year
Applications wanted here

Second's out
Second spike
People doing
What they like
Second wave
Second thought
Not doing
What we ought
Second half
Second guess
Second rate
Total mess
Second class
Second to none
Got it wrong
All along
Second chance
Not quite
Wish we had
Second sight

The Greatest Tory Ever Sold

#146 / 31:07:2020

The Bible says
Honour thy father and mother
I've changed it a bit
To honour my brother
All these commandments
From way back in time
They're so out of date
I much prefer mine

Distant

#147 / 01:08:2020

The farce that city pubs and bars
Exist with no resistance
Where masses gather freely
To drink with great persistence
Yet you cancel Eid by Twitter feed
From an anti-social distance
Insensitive at best – but ...
As usual – inconsistent

Sunday

#148 / 02:08:2020

Today, being Sunday
And traditionally being a "day of rest"
There will be no poem
Save these few words
As a child
Sundays meant church three times
No playing out down the rec
And limited television
Sunday
A day of rest
A family day
A day to pray
Today then
It is much the same
As I say a little prayer for our family
And prepare to drive to mum's
The rest of the world can wait
The rest of the week can wait
The rest of my list of things to do can wait
Today – a day of rest

The Inevitability Upon Driving to Lancashire to See Mum After Four Months of Lockdown

#149 / 03:08:2020

Inevitably
    There were tears

Inevitably
    We couldn't resist the need to embrace

Inevitably
    We felt guilty and awkward in the current climate

Inevitably
    We drove past crowded beer gardens
    Where people neither felt guilty or awkward

Inevitably

Noises Off

#150 / 04:08:2020

There's a tap-dancing albatross on my roof
Not really
Although I haven't actually checked
But it's a good opening line for a poem

Awoken early, very early
By noises off that sound like the above
Either that or the mice have hobnail boots
And are playing football with a crab apple

Early morning house silence amplifies all sound
As the squirrel with a lump hammer
Adjusts the chimney breast
And rearranges several tiles

Maybe it's not actually outside …
Perhaps there's a party in the loft
And headbanging bats are bouncing off beams
While biting the heads off jelly babies

A cup of tea later
The noises have stopped
The house has woken
And I have this poem

I go outside to welcome the day
Look up
An albatross flies off
Tap-dancing shoes fall with a percussive flourish

Early

#151 / 05:08:2020

In my back garden
The early birds are catching worms
Two magpies, a baby blackbird
And a sparrow to be exact

At the kitchen table
The early poet has finished in the bathroom
Had two rounds of toast
And is on his second cup of tea

He is also admiring his shed
The one he painted yesterday
While listening to Test Match Special
"Willow" to be exact – or light green

There is paint left over
So he is considering painting the gate
The same shade of light green
Waste not want not eh?

The early poet is catching words
And just like the paint pot
There are some left over …
Save them for another poem

Are you over seventy-five?
Isolated?
Alone?
Worried?
Confused?
In need of company?
Something to watch to while away the hours?

Good
We are here
However, because of COVID-19
We have no new programmes to speak of
Except the news of course
We are very good at that
And the news is this
Now your TV licence is no longer free

Bring Back Cash
Business Before Customers

To Be Continued

(A lyric for a song released on this date by Don Powell's Occasional Flames – reached No. 90 in the iTunes chart and is still available to download!)
#153 / 07:08:2020

All the poems I nearly wrote
All those words stuck in my throat
Every scribbled, mis-spelled note
    … to – be – con – tin – ued

All the novels that I'd planned
With characters you can understand
Fifty pages later and
    … to – be – con – tin – ued

    I'm putting off today and thinking 'bout tomorrow
    What could have been
    What should have been
    Which ideas I'm to follow
    I should be full to bursting but I'm empty and I'm hollow

All the paintings that I'd start
Original, unique and smart
Possibly great works of art
    … to – be – con – tin – ued

All responsibility –
creatively diminished
All potential masterpieces
    … remain unfinished

I'm putting off today and thinking 'bout tomorrow
What could have been
What should have been
Which ideas I'm to follow
I should be full to bursting but I'm empty and I'm hollow

Everything is all in place
And if I let it go to waste
Losing pace, losing face

    … to – be – con – tin – ued

It's time to take my chances now
Put the work in and somehow
See it through and take a bow

    … to – be – con – tin – ued

Part-Time Pop Star

#154 / 08:08:2020

Peaked at number ninety
Hovered around the hundred mark
All day and all of the night
Part-time pop stars
At one point wedged between
Mariah and Beyoncé
Oh … if only …
Part-time pop stars
Not bad for three old farts
And a glam rock pensioner
Messing about on social media
Part-time pop stars
Today – iTunes
Tomorrow – oblivion
The day after – a cup of tea and a biscuit
Part-time pop stars
Still available
As the song says
'To Be Continued'
Part-time pop stars

Today has not been a day for poetry
It has been a day for sorting the garage out
Of course, the garage has no car in it
Boxes and bags, assorted tools, bikes and … stuff
Boxes we haven't opened since we moved in
All those years ago
Bits of wood and wire that I thought might come in handy
But haven't
Although if I throw them away today
I'll no doubt need them tomorrow
Two carrier bags full of handwritten cassette tapes
That I'll never play but are full of memories
Paint I can't remember buying or using
That no longer resembles the shade on the tin anyway
Stuff, just chucked in there
Out of sight and out of mind
Until today
Today has not been a day for poetry
But Jenga with garage detritus
Rubbish has been chucked
The tumble drier has been moved
As have three bikes, one mower
Bin bags, boxes and assorted tools
All assigned new positions
Still accessible but more compact
And – with it being Sunday –
It seems it is a day of miracles …
The car is now inside the garage

I'm Getting to Quite Like My Mask

Now that you come to ask
It's not such an onerous task
You can't hear me grumble
Just a faint mumble
I'm getting to quite like my mask

When those in the street try to pass
Too rudely, too close and too fast
They don't hear the swearing
Beneath what I'm wearing
I'm getting to quite like my mask

I may look like a social outcast
But I've found a bright side – at last
No chance of lip readin'
There's a strange freedom
I'm getting to quite like my mask

Fifty–Bloody–Nine

#157 / 11:08:2020

So, I'm nearly sixty
Fifty – bloody – nine
And that is nearly SIXTY!

My maths is not deserting me
Even in these seemingly advancing years
Yes, fifty-nine

And I'm framing fifteen-pence Slade posters
From 1973 or something mad like that
Framing them!

They were never allowed on my bedroom walls at home
Mum said they would ruin the wallpaper
Dad just said they were rubbish

They briefly adorned college walls
As a statement of commitment, irony
And the fact that I could

College feels like the recent past by the way
But is nearly forty years ago
How did that happen?

Back to the Slade posters ...
They have NEVER – and I mean – NEVER
Appeared on any interior household wall during
Thirty years of married life

But now, I have a den
A room in the garage
Not in the house
And not a comment on the marriage either

It used to be my son's bolthole
PlayStation, music, cigarettes
Etcetera ...
And we all know about the etcetera ...

But now, it's been fumigated
Reclaimed, repainted, fumigated
Rearranged, fumigated
And it's mine

Desk, computer, bookshelves and books
Old magazines, concert programmes
Music, several ukuleles
And a settee – doubly fumigated

And here I am writing, typing
Creating and curating, reading, listening, hiding ...
Surrounded by a few of my favourite things
Things – my favourite people are in the house

Fifty-nine
My Slade posters are framed
They won't ruin any wallpaper
And they never were rubbish

Not an Invasion

We found them on our beaches
We found them on our sands

They came across our waters
They came from distant lands

They didn't come with malice
Or detailed battle plans

They didn't come with treaties
Ultimatums and demands

They didn't come with guns
Or weapons in their hands

They came with all the problems
We do not understand

They came with desperation
Nothing underhand

In fact they came with nothing
Each woman, child and man

An invitation-less visit …
But … it's not an invasion though, is it?

Whatever it is, this situation
Whatever it is, it's not an invasion

Take that etymology from the equation
Not an assault or attack on our nation

No onslaught that's evil or sly infiltration
No violent offensive and no violation

Maybe an act of sheer desperation
Whatever it is, it's not an invasion

Let's be clear and explicit
That's not an invasion though, is it?

Today I put my watch back on
For the first time since my own lockdown
145 days
3480 hours
208,800 minutes
12528000 seconds
Not that I've been counting
As I haven't had my watch on
I'm not even sure what the last number is
Just a number on a calculator screen
Which some readers may even go
And double-check ...
My wrist feels burdened, heavier
But it feels like it's time to move on
Reclaim some sense of normal
Even though it is clearly not the case
We have holiday weather
Feels like we are abroad
Our outlook reflects this
We are carefree – apart from shopping masks
Pubs are getting fuller
Attitudes more blasé
Social distancing is fluid and elastic
Yet there is still a death toll
Still, it feels like time to put my watch back on
Tomorrow, I may even open my diary
Although its blank pages where work once lived
Will be difficult to look at

A Statement from The Department of Education
On Behalf of The Government

#160 / 14:08:2020

Never mind the experts
Who've taught and made their mark
We know what's best to pass the test
So we'll tear it all apart
We don't want double standards
It's perfect common sense
We don't want those promoted beyond their competence

Never mind the lockdown
The problems and pandemic
Never mind that policies
Affect the academic
Never mind the work achieved
The stress that is immense
We don't want those promoted beyond their competence

Never mind the changing world
And everything uncertain
Never mind the best laid plans
Never mind the hurting
Never mind all that at all
It's our experience
We don't want those promoted beyond their competence

This isn't just a random act
But a strategy to show
We safeguard our society
Preserve the status quo
Harrow, Eton – won't be beaten
Here's the recompense
We can't have those promoted beyond their competence

Knowledge isn't privilege
It should not be a shield
To keep all those from entering
A level playing field
Equal opportunities
Not locked gates and a fence
But we can't have those promoted beyond their competence

Just look at all we've done
We know you'll all agree
All the waste on track and trace
The millions on P.P.E.
And so much more that we've ignored
We are the evidence
Of people being promoted beyond their competence

We know it's true, we know we're right
There is no pretence
We are those promoted beyond our competence

"Robust Results"

#161 / 15:08:2020

Robust results – yet standards are raided
Eton and Harrow will not be downgraded
Boundaries change as lines become shaded
Eton and Harrow will not be downgraded
Teachers' predictions are changed and then traded
Eton and Harrow will not be downgraded
Recommendations ignored and blockaded
Eton and Harrow will not be downgraded
Dreams have been shattered, hopes have all faded
Eton and Harrow will not be downgraded
Depressed and downhearted, frustrated and jaded
Eton and Harrow will not be downgraded
Are we convinced? Are we persuaded?
Eton and Harrow will not be downgraded
The truth is the truth that can't be evaded
Eton and Harrow will not be downgraded

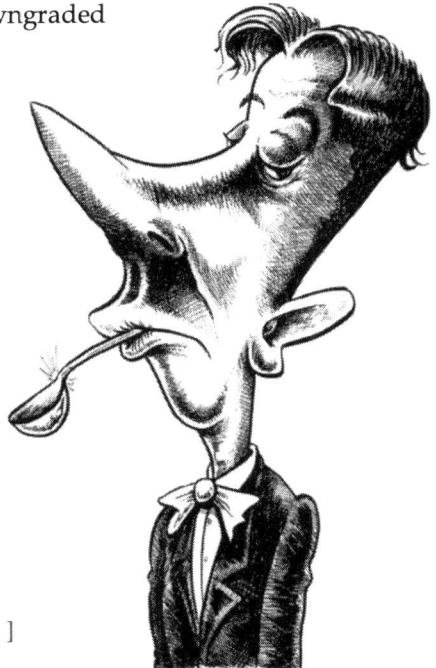

The Algorhythm Method

#162 / 16:08:2020

Today's poem has been adversely affected
By current circumstances
It was to be a much longer and adventurous poem
But has been edited to much less than its original vision

Not only that
But the *A B A B* rhyme scheme
That was to be deployed
Has now been rearranged imperceptibly

Apparently, there is nothing to be done
There are no Poetry Police
No *Serious Rhyme Squad*
Who can take this matter up

It would seem that poetic license has been revoked
And instead, there is this
Where whatever ending or punchline was in mind
Has been withdrawn, prematurely

Thanks to the algorhythm method

Put the Answers Right

(After Lord Baker of Dorking advised: "If you are in a hole, stop digging.")
#163 / 17:08:2020

The calculations that you made
Are neither fair nor just
The figures you configured
Just lead to more mistrust

If you're in a hole, stop digging
It's clear as day and night
Hold your hands up – just say sorry
Put the answers right

This chaos you created
This devastating mess
Where just what happens next
Is anybody's guess

If you're in a hole, stop digging
Look up to the light
Put down your spades, raise those grades
And put the answers right

Everybody knows it's wrong
It's obvious and clear
If it was a football match
V.A.R. is here

If you're in a hole stop digging
You can't win a losing fight
Don't attack – just backtrack
And put the answers right

You're digging your own graves
For the next election
This generation won't forget
Your un-natural selection

If you're in a hole stop digging
Before you're out of sight
Don't tell lies – apologise
And put the answers right

U Turn

#164 / 18:08:2020

You turned against the teachers
And all their expertise
You turned against the pupils
In difficult days like these
You turned against opinion
Of varying degrees
You turned – you turned – you turned
You turned opportunity
To failure not success
You turned this situation
Into un-needed stress
You turned down a chance
To do just what is best
You turned – you turned – you turned
You turned up the heat
When you could have turned it down
You turned education
Into a battleground
You turned this can of worms
Upside down and on the ground
You turned – you turned – you turned
You turned your backs on many
And chose to face the few
Now you want to turn the tide
In what you seek to do
Turn back time to change your lies
Into something true
You turned – you turned – you turned
Utterly Unfeeling
Unacceptable at best

Untrustworthy Undone
Untenable Unimpressed
Unelectable and Useless
Ungraded in this test
U failed – U failed – U failed

Prayer for the Day

#165 / 19:08:2020

May today be the day
Where hopes and dreams come true
May today be the day
Where things work out for just for you
May today be the day
That's filled with joy, not fears
May today be the day
That has no need for tears
May efforts all be recognised
Achievements celebrated
Due diligence rewarded
Paths illuminated
May today just be that day
Where the passed stay passed and so
You're looking to the future
On your marks, get set, go!

Dear Gavin

It can't have been a surprise
It's not a bolt from the blue
It's been on the cards for months now
But what did you do?
Just where was your planning?
Where was your preparation?
Your revision and working out
For this examination?

You knew this date was coming
You could have done much more
But left it all last minute
And panicked on the night before
Then realised you'd get things wrong
And without a second glance
Cancelled and delayed it all
To give yourself a second chance

Ill-prepared ineptitude
You failed at every stage
You really must try harder
If you're going to make up grades
But despite the facts in black and white
Don't worry about the shouting mob
You're with the rest who fail each test
You too can keep your job

Tom Sawyer, A Girl Called Eddy and A Boy Called Bill

#167 / 21:08:2020

'Huckleberry Unfinished'
Was going to be the witty title for this poem
As yesterday was spent painting a fence
Except it was Tom Sawyer
And he whitewashed a fence
Whereas mine is "Urban Slate" – or grey, as I like to call it
And the job is incomplete
Hence 'Huckleberry Unfinished'
Talking of names
I was joined by A Girl Called Eddy
And a boy called Bill
Companions throughout the day
I sang along to heartbreak songs
And imagined playing guitar on 'Jets at Dawn'
Should the weather be acceptable
We will reconvene, the three of us
With the "Urban Slate"
Or in this garden
"Suburban Slade"

An Important Question in the Form of a Haiku Regarding My Daily Task

#168 / 22:08:2020

a poem to write
a fence to paint – which to fin
-ish first … the poem

Covid Whispers

Shush … I haven't gone away
I haven't disappeared
Still lurking, doing my dirty work
    I'm … still … here

I may not be the front-page news
Like earlier in the year
But silence is my strength and power
    I'm … still … here

Because you all want to return
To all that you hold dear
Normality is mine
    I'm … still … here

You may be bored or weary
Forgotten all your fear
Take all the risks you want
    I'm … still … here

Ambivalence – my ally
To help me stay so near
Your laziness – my friend
    I'm … still … here

Rave on, relax, distract yourself
But let's be crystal clear
Wherever you go, whatever you do
I'll be waiting just for you
    I'm … still … here

A Breath of Fresh Air

#170 / 24:08:2020

With my first cup of tea
I stand outside my back door

Amongst other things
I admire my newly painted fence

The one that my daughter says
"Makes the grass look greener"

The wind whispers I know not what
But it is soothing

An arrogant magpie struts
One for sorrow – not as soothing

The wind, the fence, the magpie and me
And my first cup of tea

I will try to savour this moment
This peace for as long as possible

The wind may indeed whisper
But it does not lie

We Only Really Know Two Lines

#171 / 25:08:2020

Great tune, rousing finale
Gets the pulses racing
A national anthem – but better
Not sure about the words though
Don't know them all, or understand them
But those I do, I sing along with
Well, the chorus …
Don't really want to rule the waves
Don't believe in slavery
Don't believe in making slaves of others
Britain first at heaven's command
Not bothered about native oaks
Chest-beating, flag-waving, inflated pride
And national glory at the expense of others
Not really my thing
Not that we shouldn't celebrate nationality
Lots we can be proud about
Time to reclaim the Union Jack
What a tune though!
What atmosphere and passion!
Maybe it's time to rewrite the words …

And I Thought "Mutant Algorithm" Was the Latest Album by Radiohead …

#172 / 26:08:2020

Just don't blame the government
It's not our fault this time
We are the not the cause
Of this heinous cybercrime
And it wasn't OFQAL either
Who turned those grades from A to D
You can blame the MUTANT ALGORITHM
Just don't blame me

This algorithm's deadly
And its dangerous mutation
Threatening our world
Infecting education
Science fiction turns to fact
The evidence is here to see
You can blame the MUTANT ALGORITHM
Just don't blame me

This beast is out of control
A law unto itself
Constantly evolving
This monster's something else
Once a number programme
Now a living entity
You can blame the MUTANT ALGORITHM
Just don't blame me

This raging mass of numbers
These codes that ever spiral
These matrix calculations
This evil that is viral

This silent violent predator
This unseen enemy
You can blame the MUTANT ALGORITHM
Just don't blame me

It's really, really, really real
Not something we've made up
To cloud the fact we got it wrong
And put your grades back up
But somehow this thing escaped
From a strange laborat'ry
You can blame the MUTANT ALGORITHM
Just don't blame me

It Don't Mean a Thing if it Ain't Got That Swing

#173 / 27:08:2020

The Burnley Express
Jimmy Anderson – King of Swing
Unassuming hero
Ultimate professional
Metronomic guile
Fast but not furious
Intelligence and pace
Controlled aggression
Leader of the attack
Leader of the pack
Leader by example
Living legend who leads the way
Opening act yet top of the bill
Bag of tricks, sleight of hand
Twenty-two-yard magician
Wizard in dizzying spells
Mister More-than-Reliable
Numbers speak for themselves
Six hundred Test Match wickets
And still counting
The Burnley Express
Always on time
Always on the right tracks
Not over yet
Mister Anderson sir
We salute you

That Greenbelt Festival Feeling

#174 / 28:08:2020

August Bank Holiday weekend
And normally I'd be scratching that Greenbelt itch

At this point for the last forty-plus years
I would have been somewhere in a festival field
Celebrating friends and extended family
That once-a-year faithful gathering

But not today
Not me
Not any of us
Not this year when we probably need it most

I'm home with a cup of tea in hand
Looking out of the window at the pouring rain
Thinking of those annual connections
The inspiration and encouragement
The special place and special people

Fellowship of friendship
Affirmation of faithfulness
Communion of kindred spirits
The challenge of the new
Amongst the traditions of the old

So many magical moments
So many pivotal times
So many special people
Beautiful humans

The songs of those newly discovered
Who become lifelong friends
Lifelong friends and open hearts
Open hearts and restless souls
Restless souls and questions asked
Questions asked and answers offered
Answers offered and memories shared
Memories shared and cups of tea
Cups of tea and ...

Cups of tea and I'm at home
Looking at the rain
Partly glad I'm warm and safe and dry
But mostly wishing I was there and wet
Soaked in the joy of my Greenbelt gathering

Until next year my friends
Until next year
I'll put the kettle on
And think of you all and smile

Hand-Sized Biting Spiders in Your Home …
… And They're Looking for Sex

(This was an actual headline!)
#175 / 29:08:2020

There's a danger that is stranger than the truth
Amorous arachnids are descending from the roof
Guaranteed revulsion – to make you nervous wrecks
Hand-sized biting spiders in your home …
    … And they're looking for sex!

Don't be left alone when inside your empty room
Turn on all your lights and illuminate the gloom
Look behind each cushion, be careful with your checks
Hand-sized biting spiders in your home …
    … And they're looking for sex!

Fatal when they mate – beware of that attraction
You'll get so much more than a chemical reaction
Taken unawares, beware the side-effects
Hand-sized biting spiders in your home …
    … And they're looking for sex!

So seal up all the buttons on your shirts and on your blouses
Check the sheets and pillows in the bedrooms of your houses
Sellotape into your socks, the legs of all your kecks
Hand-sized biting spiders in your home …
    … And they're looking for sex!

If you feel a tickle that is rising near your thigh
Do not scream or groan – and certainly don't sigh
Some things will start to shrink as others start to flex
Hand-sized biting spiders in your home …
    … And they're looking for sex!

These eight-legged groove machines, these arthropods on heat
These swingers on their threads of lust spinning their deceit
More than just a love-bite when they peck upon your necks
Hand-sized biting spiders in your home …
     … And they're looking for sex!

Action first and fast when they start to manoeuvre
Be ready with the feather duster, ready with the hoover
Decisive and incisive – ensure they'll be an ex
Hand-sized biting spiders in your home …
     … And they're looking for sex!

Daily Prayer

#176 / 30:08:2020

Answers for the questions
Not yet asked
Solutions to problems
So far un-encountered
Respite from these burdens
Carried round so long
Strength for the weaknesses
That bring us to our knees

Wisdom and timing
To do just what is right
Grace to accept
All that is past and gone
Forgiveness to give
Healing to share
Peace in the storm
That never seems to cease

Comfort for the heart
Fragile and breaking
Solace for the soul
Troubled and alone
Sunshine for the day
Calm for the night
Belief that tomorrow
Can be a better day

Friends in a Field

#177 / 31:08:2020

Friends in a field
I have missed you
More than you can know

Lifelong histories and open hearts
Open arms and listening ears
Raucous laughter and a thousand cups of tea

Friends in a field
I have missed you
Familiar faces and kindred spirits

That field where dreams take shape
That field where souls are stirred
That field of heavenly dew

Friends in a field
Our annual family gathering
Forty-plus years of faith and fellowship

Pilgrims and travellers
At the heart of the covenant
With the art of the covenant

Yes, there is the music
And yes, there are the talks
But I think we'd all still meet if not

For we are the people
We are the festival
We are so much more than just

Friends in a field

#178 / 01:09:2020

New term
New school year
New routines
New ideas
New rules
New days
New systems
New ways
New worries
New stress
New confusion
New tests
New rooms
New signs
New work
New times
New me
New you
New beginnings
All new

#179 / 02:09:2020

A little patience
To get things just right
A little patience
As new ways are trialled
A little patience
From the pupils
A little patience
From the teachers
A little patience
From the parents
A little patience
From everyone
A little patience
To work things out
A little patience
To keep things as safe as possible
And hopefully
A little patience
Means
No little patients

Public Enema

#180 / 03:09:2020

COVID-19
Already unclean
Finding new methods to use
To spread its infection
In every direction
Wafting through pipes and up through your loos

Surfing in cisterns
And round drainage systems
Surviving the effluent ooze
Beats toilet brushes
Fighting the flushes
Wafting through pipes and up through your loos

This enemy – public
Number one – double it
Worse than the worst number twos
You can't see it coming
Invading your plumbing
Wafting through pipes and up through your loos

It will rise and ascend
From behind your U-bend
Ignoring the don'ts and the dos
However you soil it
Escaping your toilet
Wafting through pipes and up through your loos

Yes, COVID-19
In every latrine
Its tactics are meant to confuse
Craftily wafting
And draughtily drafting
Right through the pipes and up through your loos

Black and White

#181 / 03:09:2020

There are two magpies in my garden
They haven't heard the news
Or read the script
There is no joy

Oblivious to any bigger picture
They are merely early birds
Searching for worms
Trying to stay alive

Still they find the time to sing

One Hundred and Fifty-Five Days

#182 / 04:09:2020

One hundred and fifty-five days
Since I last went out to work
As in out
Out of the house
To somewhere else

One hundred and fifty-five days
Since I last faced an audience
As in live
There in front of me
Not on a Zoom screen

So here I am
Not thinking tee-shirts
But a real shirt with buttons
Trousers and actual shoes
Not slippers

I've missed my work
More than I know
The interaction, the laughter
Of audience and performer
When poetry truly lives

One hundred and fifty-five days
And I'm truly looking forward to this
Let's hope and pray that it is not
One hundred and fifty-five days
Before I get to do it all again

Nine Lines of an Average Nature
In Order to Reach a Suitable Pun

#183 / 05:09:2020

Just who is that masked man
Friend or foe or stranger
Wanting us to follow and
Wear masks to ward of danger?

Or does the mask disguise the sham
That when it all hits the fan
And we're indebted to his plan
Everyone is cap in hand
To – The Loan Arranger

The Elephant in the Room

#184 / 06:09:2020

The elephant in the room
Grows bigger day by day
The elephant in the room
That will not go away
We may have been distracted
For the best part of a year
But the mess that is Brexit is still here

The elephant in the room
Not silent for much longer
Its presence unavoidable
And influence much stronger
Murky waters muddier
Nothing crystal clear
And the mess that is Brexit is still here

The elephant in the room
That has slumbered in this past
Has lumbered into life
And is waking up at last
Minimal discussions
Repercussions that we fear
And the mess that is Brexit is still here

The elephant in the room
Has realised the powers
That could be unleashed
From its ivory towers
We could be trampled underfoot
Confusion far and near
And the mess that is Brexit is still here

No Surprise

#185 / 07:09:2020

Normality – mortality
Another number dies
And still we are ambivalent
The numbers start to rise

We seem to have forgotten
The guideline still applies
Blasé in the bars and shops
Numbers start to rise

However much you spin it
There's no way to disguise
The answers lie unfound
As the numbers start to rise

We may watch it all unfold
Before our very eyes
But it doesn't seem to register
That numbers start to rise

Negligent – not vigilant
So it can't be a surprise
That here we are again
And still the numbers rise

Recipe for Disaster

#186 / 08:09:2020

This "OVEN READY DEAL"
This soundbite that you've chosen
This turkey's past its sell by date
Plus the fact – it's frozen

The Joy of Six

#187 / 09:09:2020

Be careful how you gather
Be careful where you mix
It's the magic number
With the joy of six

You won't get your highs
You won't get your kicks
On route – or en suite
With the joy of six

Certainly no Boogie Nights
And no Ballroom Blitz
More Saturday Night Fever
With the joy of six

Less than five – stay alive
More and Covid sticks
Seven isn't heaven …
The joy of six

Act Fast?

#188 / 10:09:2020

Hands – Face – Space
Our brave Prime Minister speaks
We must act fast to save lives …
Starting from next week

I wobble and I waddle when I walk
I want to be slim and oh so sleek
Act fast – time to diet
I think I'll start next week

There's a smell of effluence
With no paddle – up this creek
Act fast – S.O.S.
Send a message out next week

There's a fire in the house
I smell the smoke and I feel the heat
Act fast – call the fire brigade
And then they can come next week

Like the Titanic and the iceberg
There seems to be a little leak
Act fast – get the lifeboats
Starting from next week

Coronavirus crisis rises
Still the numbers yet to peak
Act fast – save lives
Starting from next week

Pig's Ear, Dog's Dinner

#189 / 11:09:2020

Trade deal renegations
The hoo-ha that's in Brussels
Non negotiations
Confusing verbal tussles
Michael waves his Union Jack
And tries to flex his muscles

There's talk of cheese and chicken
Arguments on cod
Orders re soft borders
And other things most odd
Who will buy and when and why
And who will give the nod

"Trust and confidence are key"
To unlock any door
Significant differences remain
On what we're looking for
Britannia waives the rules
And sings of sovereign law

Like knitting with blancmange
Or trying to juggle with jelly
This no deal wheeler-dealing
Has left this ship unsteady
Pig's ear, dog's dinner
Far from oven ready

We get what we deserve – if we voted *Yes*
Receive our just desserts – with this Eton Mess
Led by this buffoon – failing to impress
Babbling buffoon or baffling baboon – same thing I guess

Some People Are On the Pitch ...

#190 / 12:09:2020

As football kicks off once again
The grounds are empty, now, as then
Just the sound of these few men
No volume, roar or row
We dreamed of stadia full of crowds
But alas, it's not allowed
We thought it was all over

   ... It isn't now

Instead we fans are far away
Wishing we were there today
Watching all our heroes play
And cheer along, somehow
Instead there's just the joy of six
In front of our TV sets
We thought it was all over

   ... It isn't now

Looking forward to the action
Football is the main attraction
Any positive distraction
Covid will allow
Sick of all this quarantine
We just want our football team
We thought it was all over

   ... It isn't now

It may just be a football match
A ninety-minute escape hatch
One game at once and after that
We don't know why or how
All of this will ever end
And will things be the same again?
We thought it was all over

    … It isn't now

I'm Not Used to Writing Optimistic Poems
After the First Game of a New Football Season with Everton
#191 / 13:09:2020

Same shirt – different team
Same team – different game
Same game – different football
Same football – different result

New season – old ambitions
New ambitions – old goals
New goals – old traditions
New traditions – old master

Rejected by Morrisons

#192 / 14:09:2020

That Morrisons job – long since rejected
Failed application – never selected

Time on my hands, once unexpected
A daily routine – long since neglected

A poem a day – a routine perfected
About the infected and all those affected

Or feeling let down by those we elected
A diary of thoughts and feelings dissected

All the poems later – shared and connected
Two books and counting – verses collected

Morning Moments

#193 / 15:09:2020

Were I braver and less inhibited
I would stride naked in my garden
The soles of my feet
Absorbing the life-dew diamond sheen

Days like these are numbered
Autumn temperatures will soon fall
It could be a last chance
To feel soothing sunshine warm my skin

However, being inhibited
And of a certain age and weight
The best I can do is walk to the bins
In my flip-flops and dressing gown

The sun still feels, soothes
And were the dew diamonds
Richness would be mine forever
Rather than just these morning moments

Plus, there's the neighbours to consider
Wouldn't want to traumatise them

You Give Incompetence a Bad Name

#194 / 16:09:2020

Unprecedented – maybe, but now it's been so long
We've had this situation and still you get it wrong
Not a trace of track and trace and you won't take the blame
You give incompetence a bad name

Every day's the same – you huffing, puffing, bluffing
When all is said and done – it all adds up to nothing
Hello darkness my old friend – here we are again
You give incompetence a bad name

Promises and policies – from when you were elected
The goalposts have been moved – just as we expected
The Brexit exit voted just hasn't stayed the same
You give incompetence a bad name

Bereft of moral fibre and bereft of any vision
The inconsistencies to stick to a decision
A catalogue of chances missed exist to prove this claim
You give incompetence a bad name

What next for Great Britain? We haven't got a clue
Bad news for everyone – the same is true of you
In conclusion, more confusion destined to remain
You give incompetence a bad name

Not a Trace

#195 / 17:09:2020

Let's all go to Telford
Bolton to Inverness
Not a trace of track and trace
No sign of a test

Seven weeks on Thursday
Ten thirty-five is best
Not a trace of track and trace
Cancelling the test

A pandemic that is national
North, south, east and west
Not a trace of track and trace
Try to find a test

It's not like it's surprising
So why this useless mess?
Not a trace of track and trace
No chance of a test

You can travel far and wide
Scour every single place
Discover this green pleasant land
Not a trace of track and trace

How're You Doing?

#196 / 18:09:2020

Well – you know
Good days and bad days
Actually – not true
No good days
Mostly indifferent days
Where every day feels like yesterday
And there is no new tomorrow

Sometimes a friend might ring
Or an exciting email pops up
Occasionally an interesting thread
Might distract for a while on social media
But
Mostly
It's
Boring
Or
Worse

So …
How am I doing?
Well
I'm not dead from COVID-19
But I may be dying a little bit inside
Every
Single
Day

Ode to Jacob

#197 / 19:09:2020

Oh Jacob how we've missed you
Your endless carping on
About our government so great
And the work that they have done

Oh Jacob how we've missed you
Like a soldier in our trenches
Your tireless contribution
Reclining on our benches

Oh Jacob how we've missed you
And your national civic duty
Like *Beano*'s Walter the Softy
Mutating with Lord Snooty

Oh Jacob how we've missed you
Your verbal cut and thrust
That narrow-minded bigotry
That's gained you so much trust

Oh Jacob how we've missed you
Your willingness to blame
And how your "Christian views"
Give Jesus a bad name

Oh Jacob how we've missed you
You contribute so much
Out of time and out of step
And always out of touch

Better Get Things Ready for Locktober

#198 / 20:09:2020

The numbers do not lie, there in black and white
Second wave, second spike, call it what you like
We won't be going anywhere until this is all over
Better get things ready for Locktober

Positively negative, it's getting worse again
Prepare the way for curfews and further Covid pain
I feel the need to drink a lot but maybe should stay sober
Better get things ready for Locktober

Self-isolation stakes – or there's a price to pay
With health and wealth so treat yourself and stay at home each day
No more tours to castles, no more the wild rover
Better get things ready for Locktober

No end in sight – it's just going on forever
We'd like to hope and pray that we'll get through this together
Don't know when – we'll meet again – maybe by cliffs at Dover
Better get things ready for Locktober

We Must All Have the Ability to Disagree Politely

#199 / 20:09:2020

You are all my friends
That is why we are here
There are connections
Some old, some new
But you are all connections

You are all my friends
Yet we may see things differently
Very differently at times
But that should not be a reason
For unnecessary rudeness

Not every poem I write is the truth
Sometimes just a pun, a joke
Or stretching the truth to make a point
Just an opinion

Opinions are there to be challenged
Your opinion may differ
My opinion may clash
But at the end of the day
They are opinions

You are all my friends
And if we must disagree
Let us do so with politeness
Humour and respect
Without condescension or personal attack

Poem Two Hundred

#200 / 21:09:2020

Two hundred poems
Who would have thought
That when all this started
I would have two hundred poems to show for it?

Not all good poems
Obviously
But all of them a response – at the time
And all of them honest – at the time

I keep thinking
That there'll be nothing more to write about
That it's all been said before
Then the gift that unfortunately keeps on giving

Gives again

Oh the irony
As "he" worries about money
It would be funny
If it was so hideously and seriously offensive

Unemployed, minimum wage, furloughed, ill ...
And "he" worries about hiring a nanny
Apparently, according to an un-named source
He "doesn't seem to enjoy being at the helm in rough seas"

At last
We have something in common

The Nation Watched

#201 / 22:09:2020

The Prime Minister did his best
While everyone waited for *Bake Off*

The country is in crisis
But we'd rather have *Bake Off*

It's time to get really serious about all this
But first we'll watch *Bake off*

If only *Bake Off* lasted six months
The nation would watch television

Three Things That Cheered Me Up on a Wet Wednesday

#202 / 23:09:2020

Didn't watch the news
My new book arrived early
And Everton won

If that kipper tie still fitz
And you'd like a glam rock blitz
All the glitter, all the glitz
All the mis-spelt hits and bitz
Stomp those platform boots coz itz
Slade's new Cum On Feel The Hitz

The Forgotten

#204 / 25:09:2020

Purveyors of performing arts
Who strike the right notes, lift our hearts
All of those who tread the boards
Sing the songs and play the chords

All the actors and performers
All who entertain and warm us
Those who tour, those who've played
Every venue, every stage

Those who roll, those who rock
All those folk who've had to stop
Those who gigged most every night
And now they just can not

Those who took the centre stage
Those behind the scenes who've made
All the props and all the sets
Painted backdrops and effects

Costumiers, make-up appliers
Those who lug the amplifiers
Plug in plugs, re-wire wires
Backstage drinks and food suppliers

Those who drive the vans and who
Shout in mics – one-two, one-two
Those who tune and change the strings
A million other unseen things

Those who rap and those who rhyme
Dames dressed up in pantomime
Chorus singers, all the dancers
Extras waiting for their chances

Thespians and fools and clowns
Who nightly brought those curtains down
Musicians – every style, persuasion
Every genre and occasion

Those who rock and those who roll
Lift the spirits, feed the soul
Cherish theatre and live music
If we don't protect it then we lose it

Terms and Conditions

#205 / 26:09:2020

The precedent is evident
With numbers at their peak
Holed up in halls of residence
Their future looking bleak

Isolation – education
Pay your fees – don't speak
Money's earnt – lessons learnt
Brand new term – Freshers … weak

Until Now
#206 / 27:09:2020

It's the quickest time ever
To fill a brand-new notebook
With new poems, new ideas
Lists of things to do

But mostly new poems
Regular writing
Something I've always wanted
Something I've never had time for

Until now

Because You're Worth It?
#207 / 28:09:2020

Donald's done his taxes and the fact is they are true
Seventy grand a year and that's the best that you can do?
What should be your pride of place and your crowning glory
Lawdy! Darn it! With that barnet you're the clown in every story
With that coiffure not so sure you'd survive a windy day
Is that blond mop the best you've got – or just a higher price toupee?
You put the sty in style, it's also tax deductable
At seventy grand a year it should be indestructible
You don't need a barber, a stylist or beautician
With hair like that sir what you need is Merlin the Magician

Just Another Spoke in the Unreal

#208 / 29:09:2020

Confusing for everyday folk
It's getting beyond a bad joke
When our trusted P.M.
Has blundered again
This joke of a bloke who misspoke

Positive Signs?

#209 / 30:09:2020

Today's poem is short
I've got a school visit
A positive sign of better times?
… Or is it?

Seeing It Like a Poet on National Poetry Day

("Seeing it like a poet" was this year's theme)
#210 / 01:10:2020

I've been "seeing it like a poet"
For over thirty years now
Actually, not true
Much longer than that

Writing poems for most of my life
Publishing since eighteen
Job since 1989

Not so much
"Seeing like a poet" then
My life isn't a simile
It's a fact

Seeing it as a poet
Every single day
Where every day
Is a poetry day

The Day After National Poetry Day is Still National Poetry Day

#211 / 02:10:2020

It is the day after National Poetry Day
And it is still national poetry day
As it will be tomorrow
And the day after that
And the ...

Remember
A poem is not just for
National Poetry Day
It's for life

You Can Snitch On Your Neighbour ...

#212 / 02:10:2020

If there's hot tubs and parties like *Animal House*
But not if there's guns and they're out shooting grouse

Positives are negatives – but we can make an exception
Positively negative – concerning the election

This presidential evidence … it may not be a coma
But Donald's been infected – I feel sorry for Corona

How this came to be may remain a mystery
But he's obviously more positive than anyone in history

More positively positive, the biggest virus owner
Donald's been infected – I feel sorry for Corona

Oh irony of ironies – this potential re-electant
And now it is the virus that is craving disinfectant

And bleach that will beseech, be a healer and atoner
Donald's been infected – I feel sorry for Corona

All that hate and bigotry and everything that's mean
Mutating with germs and strains in COVID-19

The outcome's looking ugly for the presidential moaner
Donald's been infected – I feel sorry for Corona

Pride that comes before a fall but not a fall from grace
For grace is not an issue – you were never in that place

Humility and dignity – for you, it's a misnomer
Donald's been infected – I feel sorry for Corona

Self-isolation – fourteen days – let's hope it's a beginning
With luck it could be longer – then everyone is winning

Now halt the Twitter feed from this serial mobile phoner
Donald's been infected – I feel sorry Corona

A nation's national health and security's been breached
Indestructible? Untouchable? This white whale has been beached

Repercussions rumble from New York to Arizona
Donald's been infected – I feel sorry for Corona

10,000

#214 / 04:10:2020

10,000's not a number to be proud of
10,000 is too many anywhere
10,000 is a number that should warn us
10,000 are the reasons to take care

10,000 are the reasons we should not be lazy
10,000 are the reasons for abiding by the rules
10,000 are the reasons for sticking to the guidelines
10,000 are the reasons to not behave like fools

10,000 are the lives that are affected
Plus the 10,000 thousand more
10,000 – the number that unites us
For what the future has in store

On the Same Page as a Certain Mister Matlock

#215 / 05:10:2020

First it was Slade, then it was Sweet
Then you and The Damned – 'Neat Neat Neat'
As past and present become complete
An ex-Sex Pistol re-tweeted my tweet

I quoted you – now it's you to repeat
The words I wrote about the elite
As punk rock and poetry meet
And an ex-Sex Pistol re-tweeted my tweet

Those in power turn up the heat
On artists as they try to compete
Live music – dead on its feet
And an ex-Sex Pistol re-tweeted my tweet

Never mind their b******s – their deceit
No surrender – no defeat
Long live the arts – our heartbeat
An ex-Sex Pistol re-tweeted my tweet

Just Not Enough

#216 / 06:10:2020

Technically speaking
We don't have children anymore
Twenty-seven and twenty
Adults

But you never stop being a parent
Ridiculously proud of their achievements
Worried by their decisions
Heartbroken at their mistakes

We may share the highs
But we also share the lows
Perhaps more so
Because we can see beyond 'the now'

Still our babies
We still want to protect them
Make the wrong things right
Take away their pain and hurt

But that is not our job anymore
Even if they let us
We may be parents
But we are powerless

And all we have is our love
And sometimes, sometimes
That love is not enough
Just not enough

Dear Mister Sunak – Hush Your Refrain

#217 / 07:10:2020

Just a thought that they ought shows total disdain
Oblivious, obviously – time and again
A lack of respect and concern that you feign
So hush your refrain that some should retrain

It isn't just stupid – but mad and insane
Ill-judged and ignorant, innately inane
As anyone knows who's got half a brain
So hush your refrain that some should retrain

So out of touch and yet still you claim
That you understand the stress and the strain
Your platitudes drip like rain down a drain
So hush your refrain that some should retrain

Just tell us again – just try to explain
The logic within – just what will it gain?
How can this help? Just what is your aim?
So hush your refrain that some should retrain

Art's at the heart of everything sane
So keep your mouth shut, let your head hang in shame
Hush your refrain that some should retrain
Perhaps all of you should do just the same

Living the Retraining Scheme Dream

Stormzy is serving in Subway
Adele's on the checkout at Asda
Ed Sheeran is now a lollipop man
Stopping the cars driving faster

Take That are delivery drivers
Dua Lipa is now a barista
Paloma Faith is now the new face
At Boots selling stuff to your sister

Jagger and Richards – a firm you can trust
For all your botanical needs
Jeff Lynne and Co. – the new E.L.O.
Electric Light Offers in Leeds

Ozzy is now in the priesthood
His confessions are better than yours
Macca's a driver for SAGA
Organising OAP tours

Harry has opened his new "Hairy Styles"
Morrisey's serving in Greggs
Bono's now a beautician
Doing back, sack and crack with The Edge

The Arctic Monkey's deliver to Iceland
Tom Jones is at B&Q
So is Rod Stewart and Brian May
Cliff Richard is helping out too

Phil Collins is now a chauffeur here and there
His car – he'll expertly park it
Lewis Capaldi is managing Aldi
Sting's selling pants down the market

Little Mix now serve fish and chips
Not really got the X-Factor
Shirley Bassey is looking less classy
On her Massey Ferguson tractor

Boy George is building up burgers
On an M62 service station
Shane McGowan's a railway announcer
Messing up your destination

Olly Murs now works in healthcare
Clapton is now a mechanic
Elton has got his barbers
Now there's a reason to panic

The Gallagher brothers are plumbers
Do you really want them near your drain?
Rishi is singing the blues
It's what happens when we all retrain

Friday's Poem Is Often Short
Because It's the Day I Do My Weekly Shop

#219 / 09:10:2020

The crisis of Covid continues
The numbers they rise as we speak
But Boris won't panic about the pandemic
He'll make an announcement next week

Moving the Goalposts

#220 / 10:10:2020

I started off thinking "when"
Now it's more like "if"
More often than not these days …
"Never"

And even though it's nothing to do with football
I long for the words of Kenneth Wolstenholme

They think it's all over …
It is now

Covid that is
Not the world

#221 / 11:10:2020

Rainy Saturday
Heavy hearts
Daughter leaves
Term starts

Uncertain times
Distant parts
Isolation
Term starts

Numbers rise
Covid charts
Fear factor
Term starts

Coronavirus
Dark arts
Troubled waters
Term starts

Love is strong
Far apart
Daughter leaves
Term starts

Poem for a Monday

#222 / 12:10:2020

A poem for a Monday
Should try and give hope
At the beginning of a new week

A poem for a Monday
Should do something to allay
The so-called oft-quoted blues

A poem for a Monday
Should not be manic
But do something positive

So, today – this Monday
Phone your family
Tell them that you love them

Text a friend
With something uplifting
Smile at a stranger two metres away

And you can be the poem
The living poetry in motion
For a Monday

And every day

Today Demands a Poetic Response
Much More Serious Than the One
That Springs to Mind …

#223 / 13:10:2020

We are told – we must be brave
As winter looms – looking grave
Everyone's a loser when it comes down to this lockdown

Puns and clichés sally forth
Ee bah gum – it's grim oop north
And all we seem to get are the Tiers of a Clown

PIG'S EAR, DOG'S DINNER

PAUL COOKSON

A COVID POETRY DIARY VOL3
illustrated by Korky Paul

Summer 2021